WHAT MAKES A VAN GOGH A VAN GOGH?

Richard Mühlberger

The Metropolitan Museum of Art
Viking
NEW YORK

VIKING
Published by the Penguin Group, Penguin Putnam Books for Young Readers, 345 Hudson Street, New York, New York 10014.

Paperback edition published in 1993 by The Metropolitan Museum of Art and Viking, a division of Penguin Books USA Inc.
Hardcover edition published in 2002 by The Metropolitan Museum of Art and Viking, a division of Penguin Putnam Books for Young Readers.

10 9 8 7 6 5 4 3 2 1

Produced by the Department of Special Publications, The Metropolitan Museum of Art: Series Editor, Mary Beth Brewer; Cover Design, Anna Raff; Design, Nai Y. Chang.

The Library of Congress has cataloged the paperback edition as follows:

Mühlberger, Richard. What makes a van Gogh a van Gogh? / Richard Mühlberger.
   p. cm.
"The Metropolitan Museum of Art."
Summary: Explores such art topics as style, composition, color, and subject matter as they relate to twelve works by van Gogh.
ISBN 0-87099-673-8 (MMA pbk.) ISBN 0-670-85198-1 (Viking pbk.)
1. Gogh, Vincent van, 1853–1890—Criticism and interpretation—Juvenile literature. 2. Painting, Dutch—Juvenile literature. 3. Impressionism (Art)—Netherlands—Juvenile literature. [1. Gogh, Vincent van, 1853–1890. 2. Painting, Dutch. 3. Art appreciation.] I. Metropolitan Museum of Art (New York, N.Y.) II. Title.
ND653.G7M85 1993 759.9492—dc20 93-7582 CIP AC

ISBN 1-58839-024-1 (MMA) ISBN 0-670-03573-4 (Viking)

Printed in Italy

ILLUSTRATIONS
Unless otherwise noted, all works are by Vincent van Gogh and in oil on canvas.

CONTENTS

At boarding school, thirteen-year-old Vincent was not sociable. His sister wrote that he had a head of reddish hair and eyes that were blue or green "according to his changing expressions." His brow, she reported, "was already slightly wrinkled, his eyebrows drawn together in deep thought."

Meet Vincent van Gogh

Vincent Willem van Gogh was born on March 30, 1853, in the Dutch village of Groot-Zundert, near the Belgian border. His father, the son of a minister, was a minister himself. From his father's side of the family, Vincent inherited a deep respect for humanity, while his mother passed on to him her love of art and nature. Pastor and Mrs. van Gogh made great sacrifices to send their three daughters and three sons to good schools. Vincent, the oldest, was the first to go away. He was eleven at the time and was sad to leave home. He was an average student but worked very hard, and by the age of thirteen was studying Dutch, German, French, and English, as well as arithmetic, history, geography, botany, zoology, calligraphy, and gymnastics. He also took drawing lessons. But in March of 1868, Vincent abruptly returned home and spent a year with his parents, and then decided not to finish school. He was sixteen years old when he left home to earn a living.

His first job was in an art gallery. Next he became a schoolteacher, and then, following in his father's footsteps, he became a minister. He chose to work in a desperately poor mining district, where he suffered great poverty but found solace in making drawings of the miners. After about two years, Vincent was convinced that he was meant to serve humanity through art. From that moment, he never stopped drawing and painting.

During his short life, van Gogh earned almost no money at all and depended on an allowance that his brother Theo sent him. Vincent wrote many letters to Theo, whom he loved deeply, and it is from them that so much is known of Vincent's life and art.

This book begins in 1885, when van Gogh painted his first large canvas, a personal triumph after almost five years of continuous study and practice. It shows the unusual subject of a peasant family eating potatoes. Van Gogh wrote to his brother that what he tried most was "to bring life into it." As you follow van Gogh's brief journey on these pages, you will see that his remarkable style brought life into everything he painted.

The Potato Eaters

Van Gogh's First Masterpiece

Vincent van Gogh was thirty-two years old when he painted his first masterpiece. In preparation for the painting, he had spent an entire winter drawing pictures and painting small studies of the stolid, hardworking peasants of the poor region where he lived. Van Gogh wrote to his brother Theo, "By witnessing peasant life continually, at all hours of the day, I have become so absorbed in it that I hardly ever think of anything else." Van Gogh became friends with one peasant family, the De Groots. In their grimy, thatch-roofed cottage, van Gogh was inspired to try to paint a picture larger and more important than any he had done before.

The magical way the flickering flame of a lamp illuminated the dark interior of the De

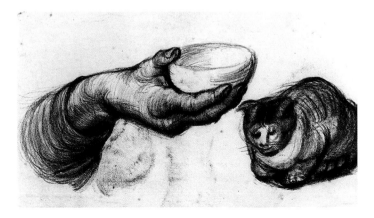

HAND WITH BOWL AND CAT

Groots' cottage fascinated van Gogh. The flame made objects and people in the darkness visible, something he would attempt with paint. While van Gogh studied the dim light from the flame, he also saw how his friends lived. He decided that his painting would show the entire De Groot family around a table under the lamp, with a platter of steaming potatoes before them.

To memorize how the De Groots looked and acted, van Gogh made dozens of paintings and sketches of their heads and hands. The De Groots were patient with their artist friend, and all winter through, allowed him to make oil studies of them by day whenever he found them not working, and drawings by night. Finally, he felt he could paint them from memory.

Earth Colors and Colorful White

Describing one of his oil studies, van Gogh said it was "painted with earth." That was the feeling it had. But, as a matter of fact, some of the pigments that he used are called earth colors because they come from clay, rocks, and mineral deposits. Van Gogh had studied seventeenth-century Dutch paintings, in which dark, earthy colors with touches of white were often used. He wanted his paintings to look like them.

Actually, most of the white seen in *The Potato Eaters* is not white at all. Pure white would have been too bright in the dark room. It is a light gray that looks like white because it is lighter than any other color in the painting. Only to paint highlights did van Gogh use small touches of pure white.

Making People Bigger Than Life
Van Gogh painted *The Potato Eaters* in a small bedroom that he rented as a studio from the care-taker of the local Catholic church; he slept in an even smaller space in the attic. His studio was almost as dark as the room in the painting. When he was unsure of a detail as he worked, he would tuck the canvas under his arm and hurry to the De Groots' cottage.

The De Groots' arms and legs are longer in

THE POTATO PEELER

PEASANT WOMAN COOKING BY A FIREPLACE

the painting than they were in real life; if the painted family all stood up, they would be noble giants. Van Gogh extended their limbs to give these kind peasants greater importance, just as artists of old did with figures of saints. Van Gogh also exaggerated their facial features to emphasize their inner strength. These stalwart farmers communicate care and affection for one another without speaking.

Simple Pleasures

Potatoes must have been boring for the De Groots, since they ate them every day. But they surely looked forward to sipping the freshly brewed coffee that is here poured with simple ceremony. Van Gogh shows how much they appreciate the drink by picturing one of the men eagerly holding up his cup and the second man looking up from the potatoes to the aromatic treat across the table. The potatoes may represent the earthbound monotony of peasant life, but the coffee represents its simple pleasures.

As van Gogh worked on his masterpiece, he became more interested in the De Groots than in the flame of the lamp. He shrouded unnecessary details in shadows so that each face seems as much a light in the dark room as the lamp is. This was van Gogh's way of showing the dignity of these farmers whom he so greatly respected.

With growing confidence in himself, van Gogh left Holland to study painting in Antwerp, Belgium, where he learned to use brighter colors.

But after three months there, he was still a Dutch painter of solid facts. What now interested him were the aims of a group of young painters in Paris who captured the fleeting impressions of light. His brother Theo lived there and was friendly with many of these new artists, so Vincent decided to join him and moved to Paris in 1886.

Soon after van Gogh painted the De Groot family, he wrote, "I like so much better to paint the eyes of people than to paint cathedrals." The eyes were generally regarded as windows to the soul; to van Gogh, a painting of a face was as spiritual as a painting of a church.

THE POTATO EATERS

The Potato Eaters *was van Gogh's driving interest from early April until*
May 6, 1885, when he completed it. He never spent so many days on a picture
again, but this was his first important work, and he wanted to make a big
impression with it.

Self-Portrait with Gray Felt Hat

Painting with Dots and Dashes of Color

In Paris, van Gogh painted more than twenty self-portraits, and in only two early ones did he feature the earth colors of his native Holland. After he met a young artist named Paul Signac, van Gogh filled the backgrounds of his self-portraits with lively colors and patterns.

Signac was ten years younger than van Gogh, but that did not keep them from becoming friends and going to the country together on painting excursions. Signac had learned a new method of painting that was to become known as pointillism. In pointillism, small dots, or points, of unmixed color were dabbed onto the canvas next to one another so they would appear to blend when a viewer stepped back from the painting.

Figuring out the color of each dot required some knowledge of color theory, and van Gogh had no patience with mixing science and art. But when he saw the beautiful paintings that resulted from pointillism, he adopted what Signac taught him. Even with Signac coaching him, though, van Gogh would not paint an entire canvas with dots. Signac kept trying to get him to do it; van Gogh kept making his dots into dashes. But to make his young friend feel better, van Gogh painted the sleeves of a blue work shirt with little dots of color and wore it when he went painting with Signac.

Painting the Modern Way

In *Self-Portrait in Front of an Easel*, painted early in 1888 and one of van Gogh's last Parisian self-portraits, the artist remembered what Signac taught him but added much more from his own imagination. Here, he even depicts his palette with short dashes of color on it. In *Self-Portrait with Gray Felt Hat*, the dabs and dashes of color follow the curving surfaces of van Gogh's face and shoulders, as well as the outline of his head and upper body. As Signac promised van Gogh, from a distance the dabs and dashes blend into colors that look like the actual colors of the things he painted—van Gogh's face, hair, clothing, and hat. Up close, though, they seem to depict a carnival mask.

Paul Signac
THE JETTY AT CASSIS
Paul Signac's enthusiasm for painting with small dots of color awakened van Gogh's appreciation for modern ways of expressing himself. He preferred bigger and bolder patterns, but enjoyed experimenting with the method his young friend used in paintings like this one.

SELF-PORTRAIT IN FRONT OF AN EASEL

Although he cast a shadow across almost his entire face, van Gogh painted his beard so it seems to glow from within by putting orange and blue near each other. This contrast emphasizes both colors, just as the squared corners of the stretched canvas and palette bring out the curves of the head and shoulders.

SELF-PORTRAIT WITH GRAY FELT HAT

The patterns of short, colorful lines radiating from his eyes and circling his head are done in van Gogh's very own new style. He eventually devised other ways to paint portraits, reserving broken patterns for landscapes, but for the moment, this self-portrait proved that he had become a modern artist at last.

Portrait of Père Tanguy

When van Gogh first arrived in Paris, he knew no one but his brother, but that was to change quickly. On his second day in the city, van Gogh met Julien Tanguy, who had an art-supply shop midway between Theo's art gallery and the apartment the two van Gogh brothers shared. Artists found Julien Tanguy kind and generous, and they affectionately called him Père ("father") Tanguy.

It was at Père Tanguy's cramped store that van Gogh had met Paul Signac and many other artists. The shop was a place to learn new ideas. Tanguy liked art that was not traditional, and he sold paintings that were different and unusual. Van Gogh decided to honor him by painting his portrait. He showed the kind man with his hands folded on his lap, his eyeglasses neatly tucked into his jacket pocket. Behind him, the wall is papered with Japanese prints.

When van Gogh painted the portrait, he had been collecting Japanese prints for two years. Eventually he owned hundreds like the ones that cover the wall behind Père Tanguy. Tanguy himself apparently did not collect these exotic works of art, nor did he sell them in his shop; perhaps they are behind him in the portrait simply to express his great love of art. They also serve as a lively contrast to this solid paint merchant.

Tanguy is posed exactly in the center of the canvas, his left side almost perfectly balancing his right side. Above him is a print of Japan's famous Mount Fuji. The neckline of Tanguy's coat and its lapels are three **V** shapes, each like the sacred mountain. The angle between his legs also repeats the shape of Fuji. The other prints behind him do not echo his pose; instead, they show flowers, people, and a landscape, subjects that van Gogh loved to paint.

Van Gogh's Hobby

Japan became van Gogh's hobby. He read everything he could get his hands on about the country and its art, and was convinced that Japan was the ideal society. To bring himself closer to the great artists of Japan, he made careful, painted copies of a few of the most dramatic Japanese prints he could find.

The prints behind Père Tanguy were cheaply made in Japan and came to Paris as packing material in crates of merchandise. Once artists saw their bold colors, strong outlines, and unusual perspectives, they wanted to use these devices in their own art. Before long, the throwaway prints were being collected.

Sunflowers

On to Arles

It was the coldest month of 1888 when van Gogh left Paris for the south of France, where the sun was brighter and where he hoped to find warmer days and clearer skies. The artist's destination, the ancient town of Arles, became his home for almost fifteen months. While he was there, he enjoyed the most productive period of his life, painting nearly two hundred canvases and making more than a hundred drawings and watercolors. "I go on like a painting locomotive," he said, describing his fervent activity.

When he arrived in Arles, van Gogh knew no one, but he liked the place well enough to search for a house where he could live and paint. After a few months, he rented one he could afford on the outskirts of town near the railroad station, and he lived in various hotels while painting and furnishing his new domain. Van Gogh's house was across from a public garden where oleanders grew. Sunflowers edged the railroad tracks, and golden fields of wheat stretched to low-lying hills in the distance, inviting the artist to walk and to paint.

Golden Flowers

In his letters to Theo, van Gogh commented enthusiastically on how beautifully nature combines the blue of the sky with the yellow of the fields. He envisioned six paintings of sunflowers to decorate his house, describing them as "a symphony in blue and yellow." The "raw chrome yellows [of the sunflowers] will blaze forth" against the blues, he wrote.

VINCENT'S HOUSE

In making this record of his new surroundings in Arles, van Gogh painted the little four-room house where he lived against the bluest of skies. He knew the colors would intensify one another.

OPPOSITE:
SUNFLOWERS

Van Gogh first found sunflowers on the edge of Paris, where city and country met, and he painted this detailed view of them. The spiky dried petals, each reaching separate ways, contrast with the evenly packed center of seeds.

Cut sunflowers wilt quickly, so van Gogh rose at dawn to gather enough flowers for a painting, and then would "do the whole in one rush." The rest of the day, he painted other subjects. He wanted to finish enough sunflower paintings to brighten the guest room and studio of his house in time for a visit by Paul Gauguin, an artist friend whom van Gogh greatly admired. He completed at least four sunflower paintings by the time Gauguin arrived. His guest loved them, and even made a portrait of van Gogh painting a canvas filled with the yellow flowers.

Painting Light on Light

In this painting of sunflowers, a thin blue line separates the dark table from the pale wall and enlivens the yellow tones. There is also a blue line around the belly of the vase that serves as a border between the areas of dark and pale yellow. Van Gogh added touches of blue to the bottom and left side of the vase, too. In painting golden flowers against a yellow background, van Gogh said he was dealing with "light on light." To van Gogh, yellow represented the sun.

Energy and Motion

In van Gogh's exuberant depiction of them, the fifteen sunflowers take on individual personalities. Each one is a slightly different size, and some are laden with petals while others are losing them. The six fattest flowers, down the center of the picture, are formed by clusters of small, thick dabs of dark orange paint, making them look like seed balls almost ready to burst. The other sunflowers extend orange and green tendrils. These curled and jagged lines appear to be in constant wavelike motion, and they fill the spaces between blossoms, animating the bouquet.

The vase is divided into two sections, contrasting with the two colors of the background. The top is brightly colored, so it stands out against the yellow wall. The bottom is pale yellow, making it stand out against the dark tabletop. In proper Japanese style, nothing in the painting casts a shadow. This makes the bottom of the vase look as flat as the wall behind it.

Sunflowers is as much a symbolic painting as it is a celebration of nature's bounty. Almost two years after he painted the sunflower series, in a letter to his sister Willemien, van Gogh said that the flowers "may symbolize gratitude." At the time he painted them, his heart was full of thanks to his brother for his support, to Gauguin for his friendship, and to the sun for its light and warmth.

Van Gogh's dream to decorate his house entirely with sunflower paintings might seem too much of a good thing, but his scheme was to vary each painting. Backgrounds would be yellow or blue, combinations he believed would provide endless visual stimulation. After a few were painted, he decided yellow against yellow looked best, and he stuck to it.

The Café Terrace at Night

A Friendly Café

Cafés are usually lively, sociable places, and they were beloved by the artists of the nineteenth century. As the word café indicates, coffee is served there, as well as other drinks and light meals. For the artists in van Gogh's day, conversation was the main course, provided by the faithful clientele. (Some went so regularly that their mail was delivered there.) Van Gogh knew of a stylish café in the center of Arles where patrons sat outdoors at night, and he went there to paint this picture.

In the painting, van Gogh created three kinds of light. A gas lamp reaches out from the café wall on a bracket and emits an intense yellow radiance. The underside of the awning bounces its reflection back to the tabletops and out onto the street. A second, softer light comes from the windows and doors. To create this light, van Gogh scattered patches of orange throughout the canvas. The largest of these are the windows and doors of the café itself and of the corner shop across the street. The third kind of light comes from the stars in the heavens, some of which van Gogh painted with strokes of luminous silver to suggest the way real stars shine. The tables on the terrace below almost seem to be their reflections.

The Richly Colored Night

Small figures under the awning are silhouetted against areas of lively color. The diagonal lines made by the ruts in the cobblestones, the edges of the awning, the orange terrace, and the slant of the doors and window in the café wall all lead to them. A man enters the café. A waiter is ready to take an order. Customers sit beneath the dazzling light from the gas lamp as it makes the colors of the walls and the street glow. In the walls, yellow shifts to orange and green. The pavement stones are lavender, purple, blue, yellow, orange, and even a little pink. "The night is more alive and more richly colored than the day," van Gogh wrote to Theo. He was proud of painting "a night picture without any black, nothing but beautiful blue and violet and green." His enthusiasm for the colors shows in the generous way he applied them. Even in a reproduction, his thick brushstrokes are apparent across the underside of the awning and in the deep green pine branches opposite it.

Although it is late at night in the city, van Gogh used bright colors to depict the café terrace. The darkest areas are made up of deep blue, green, and purple. Nowhere can pure black be found. His artist friends in Paris taught him that even shadows are composed of a mixture of colors.

Harvest at La Crau

A Sea of Fields

In June and July of 1888, van Gogh took many walks into the countryside around Arles. He told his sister that he looked like a dusty porcupine on these excursions, with his easel, canvases, paints, "and other merchandise" bristling out from across his shoulders and back, under his arms, and dangling from both hands. La Crau is three miles northeast of Arles, and van Gogh made about fifty outings to this area, painting and drawing the fields and farm buildings. Although *Harvest at La Crau* looks tranquil, van Gogh was fighting strong, steady winds as he painted it. "The canvas was shaking all the time," he wrote. There were also pesky mosquitoes. "If a view makes you forget these annoyances, it must have something in it," he stated.

Van Gogh found the fields of La Crau to be "as beautiful and as infinite as the sea." He wanted to memorize the terrain, for he had something special in mind. He did not want to picture it from ground level, for that would prevent him from showing how the fields seem to go on endlessly. He wanted the same sense of infinity captured in the sweeping landscape vistas painted by his seventeenth-century countryman Jacob van Ruisdael. In van Ruisdael's paintings, scenes were viewed from on high. Having studied the territory from ground level, van Gogh imagined it from an elevated vantage point and painted it that way. The high perspective made the fields seem to go on much farther than van Gogh could actually see as he wandered through them.

Jacob van Ruisdael
WHEATFIELDS

The Blue Cart

Van Gogh wanted to lead the viewer's eye quickly from the foreground of the painting to the background. He did this by careful planning. Long strokes of the brush at the bottom of the

THE BLUE CART (DRAWING)

canvas rush the eye to two small fields. On the edge of these plots of land, a blue cart commands the very center of the painting. Its long harnessing poles and the fence beside it direct the eye back and forth across the canvas before allowing the viewer to explore the green and yellow fields beyond. Van Gogh bordered the fields with lines that quickly lead to the abandoned monastery and to the low mountains in the distance. At the end of that summer, van Gogh decided that this painting was the best thing he had done.

Van Gogh created textures with his Japanese pen that he did not attempt to imitate with his paintbrush. The painting shows the variety of vegetation through different colors, while a drawing of the same subject uses dots, dashes, squiggles, and different patterns of parallel lines.

The Bedroom

A House and Bedroom All His Own

When van Gogh could afford to furnish his house, he selected simple pieces for his bedroom and fancier ones for the guest room. The four-room building was the closest thing he had in his entire life to a home of his own. Gauguin was coming to visit, and van Gogh fancied that other artists would soon flood to Arles. His home would be "the studio of the south." In addition to the sunflower paintings, he planned to hang other works so Gauguin could see what he had been doing. A painting of his bedroom would be among them.

Van Gogh approached the project with zest. He made two drawings of the room, and "thought out loud" in a long letter to Theo about the colors he would use, which he felt should suggest sleep and "rest the brain." When he finished the painting, it pleased him so much that he made a copy of it for his sister Willemien and his mother.

Jarring Colors and Outlines

Van Gogh confessed that it was not easy "to achieve simplicity with garish colors." One way he did this was by using large areas of flat colors—blue, green, yellow, lavender, and red. These jarring hues made familiar things stand out. He had other ways of doing this as well. Every piece of furniture is outlined in black or dark brown for emphasis. By not using shadows under them, van Gogh made the furniture appear flat, just as things looked in Japanese prints. The pieces almost seem to float above the floor. He sloped the floor itself so that the right side is higher than the left, and the rear wall slants back from the bed. All this makes for a somewhat topsy-turvy place; only the furniture looks stable. In contrast to the room, the furniture has "a familiar and reassuring spirit" that van Gogh said makes repose possible.

Empty Chairs and Other Symbols

The little nightstand is tidily set up for van Gogh's use. There is soap in a dish, a pitcher and glass for water, another pitcher and bowl for bathing, two bottles, and a hairbrush. The brightest spot in the painting is the mirror above the nightstand. A dash of white makes it stand out against the wall. A coarse linen towel with a narrow red inner border hangs from a nail next to the door. The two chairs, their rush seats slanting as the floor does, and the two fluffy pillows on the bed might be symbols of van Gogh's constant wish for someone to share his life.

Interior views were a Dutch tradition in which an artist showed off his knowledge of perspective in painting the floorboards and walls. Van Gogh invented his own system of perspective to make his bedroom inviting. Instead of carrying the viewer back to the far wall, van Gogh's floor seems to pause at each piece of furniture.

For hundreds of years, Western artists have used symbols established in classical and Christian traditions. Van Gogh's symbols, however, were very personal, emerging from his deepest thoughts and hopes. As a student away from home, he wept at the sight of an empty chair used by his father during a visit. To van Gogh, empty chairs symbolized absence and death.

Van Gogh painted no portraits of Paul Gauguin, but he did paint the chair Gauguin used during his visit. Van Gogh also made a painting of his own chair as a mate to the painting of Gauguin's. The chairs stand in opposing directions, each one viewed from above. In *Gauguin's Chair*, the green and yellow of its striped seat unite the curved and spreading lines with the blurred patterns of the carpet. *Van Gogh's Chair* has lines as straight as the edge of the door behind it, and it is as rustic as the pattern of the simple floor tiles. Van Gogh said

GAUGUIN'S CHAIR

Van Gogh had an instinct for making objects fit into their environment. He linked Gauguin's chair to the carpet pattern by changing the rush seat from its natural yellow color to green.

28

that *Gauguin's Chair* included two novels and a lighted torch "in the absent one's place." Perhaps the "torch"—actually a candle—was lighting the way for Gauguin's return. A lighted candle is also an ancient symbol of life and resurrection. The gas lamp on the wall is ablaze, creating rich bluish-purple shadows on the opposite side of the chair and making it clear that this is a night scene. One of the chair's legs extends beyond the bottom edge of the canvas.

Van Gogh's Chair was painted in daylight and takes up just about as much space as the painting of Gauguin's chair. Van Gogh's pipe and an open package of tobacco are part of the still life. Stored on the red tile floor are onions in a wooden box. Van Gogh shows a corner of it, a space just large enough for his signature. This close-up painting of his chair seems to express the feelings of comfort and rest he derived from the sturdy, simple furniture he owned in Arles.

VAN GOGH'S CHAIR
(THE CHAIR AND THE PIPE)

Van Gogh connected his chair to the room by making the thin yellow line on the door touch the top of one of the chair legs. He also repeated the pattern where the sections of the seat come together at the intersections of the floor tiles.

L'Arlésienne

A Fast Masterpiece

With the fields dormant, van Gogh turned to portraiture during the winter months. He painted about forty, all of neighborhood people, including Madame Ginoux, who, with her husband, operated a café near his house. Madame Ginoux posed for van Gogh and Gauguin at about the same time. Gauguin captured the dignified woman's face from the front, while van Gogh preferred to pose her turned a little away from him so he could see the broad band of her headdress trailing to the back of the chair. Probably at the artist's request, Madame Ginoux dressed in a traditional costume of Arles, and hence today the painting is called *L'Arlésienne*, or "the woman of Arles." She was van Gogh's friend, and he had known her long enough to realize that sitting still made her nervous. He obliged her by "slashing on" the paint in less than an hour's time.

"Black, black, black, with perfectly raw Prussian blue," was van Gogh's description of the color of his model's costume. The green table on which Madame Ginoux leans is very dark, too. These deep tones in front of the citron yellow wall make her stand out like a raven against the sun. The pages of the book and the collar of Madame Ginoux's dress are mint green. Van Gogh avoided white because it would have been too bright against the dark colors.

Exaggerated Shapes

The scalloped silhouette of Madame Ginoux's headdress delighted van Gogh, and he found similar contours in the profile of her sleeves. The shape of the arm of the chair, only partially shown, is echoed in the yellow space under Madame Ginoux's right arm. Her face is brought to life with dabs of red on her eyelids and lips. The same red outlines parts of her hand and defines the pretty embroidery on her long collar. The orange that van Gogh used to paint one of the books in front of Madame Ginoux is repeated in the chair back. The books are not just props. They elevate the portrait from one of a woman at rest to one of an intelligent reader musing over the pages before her.

Months after van Gogh painted Madame Ginoux's portrait, he became ill. In a fit of depression, he sliced off his earlobe. Certain that van Gogh was dangerous, Gauguin quickly returned to Paris, and many of the people of Arles turned their backs on him as well. Fearing he was going mad, van Gogh entered a mental hospital. He was never to enjoy life in his own house again.

Van Gogh found landscapes and still lifes easier to paint than figures. But he believed that the public would be won over to modern art through portraits, so he worked hard to compose them in unusual and interesting ways.

Cypresses

Flames of Green

Van Gogh's new home was an asylum in an old priory in the mountain foothills outside the town of Saint-Rémy. He described the place as a "rest home" and assured his brother, "I'm all right here. . . . The fear of madness has largely fallen from me now that I see around me those afflicted with it." He had spells when he could not paint, yet still he managed to complete more than one hundred magnificent canvases and one hundred drawings during his year-long hospitalization.

The terrain around Saint-Rémy was more rugged than the flat plains of Arles, and van Gogh was particularly drawn to the tough cypress trees that abounded there. They reminded him of Egyptian obelisks in their fine proportions and beauty. They "are always occupying my thoughts," he wrote. "I would like to make something of them like the canvases of the sunflowers, because it astonishes me that they have not been done as I see them." But after he tried, he complained that he had not been able "to do them as I feel them." He did not give up, and in his painting *Cypresses*, he was finally able to express the strong emotion that gripped him in front of nature.

The cypress has many small, dark evergreen needles that grow close together. Van Gogh described the color as a "difficult bottle-green hue." In his painting, the trees are tinged with a yellowish green, and lavender and blue limbs show through the blanket of needles. Van Gogh applied the paint with curving and spiraling brushstrokes. The luscious strokes of color are so thick that there are ridges and valleys everywhere on the surface of the canvas. This thickly applied paint forms a landscape of its own when viewed close up.

Van Gogh often pictured two cypress trees so close together that they practically seem to grow out of a single trunk. Here, shrubs mask the base of the smaller tree. Van Gogh painted the taller cypress rising beyond the top of the canvas, which makes it seem even larger than it is. Twisting and turning, the trees are shaped like great flames, and the ground, the mountains, and the brambles below echo their spiraling play. Dots and dashes of paint scurry through the sky, which is filled with tumbling pink clouds and a thin crescent moon. It is impossible to find a straight line anywhere in the painting.

Swirls Everywhere

Van Gogh used drawings in a number of ways. When he was learning the appearance of a place

Van Gogh fit patterns into every square inch of this painting. The twisting marks of his brush endow the work with rhythm and energy.

In van Gogh's drawings, light is represented by the paper itself, so he always had to plan where not to put ink. The darkest areas are where he placed thick lines closest together. To avoid mistakes, he usually drew the scene in pencil first.

or thing, drawing was his aid. He also drew pictures in his letters to his family and friends to show them what he was painting. Other drawings were copies of his paintings, which he would either keep as records or give away. He made drawings, too, as works of art in themselves, not as preparations for paintings or records afterward. It was less expensive to make a drawing than a painting, because the materials were simpler. His reed pen, like the ones Japanese artists used, fitted into his shirt pocket, and he could carry his ink and drawing pad in one hand.

In van Gogh's drawing of the pair of cypress trees, he invented two ways of filling his landscape with motion. He formed his trees entirely of swirls, and the brambles and mountains are all heaving, curving lines. In the painting, he simplified these two designs into the one swirling pattern that fills the canvas. Just as he learned to make patterns with dots and dashes when he lived in Paris, he now turned what he saw into swirls. By filling heaven and earth with such animated and colorful energy, van Gogh found a unique way to express his awe at the fullness of creation.

Wheatfield

The Starry Night

To paint or draw a subject, van Gogh had to have it right in front of him. Gauguin encouraged him to compose paintings from his imagination, but he found that very difficult. Even when he was confined to his room in the hospital at Saint-Rémy, he painted what he could see out the window. He seems never to have gotten bored with the restricted view of the landscape through his window and its iron bars. There was a sloping field, an enclosing wall, three farm buildings that van Gogh could see only partially, and a mountain ridge beyond. He captured every detail of this scene in rain and shine.

Van Gogh's way of painting suddenly changed, at least for the moment. A religious subject came to his mind and he felt compelled to paint it. At last, he had an idea in his mind's eye that he could transfer to paper and canvas. The result was *The Starry Night*. He never described it in his letters or said what the subject was about, so the meaning of the painting is personal and secret.

The painting shows a sky alive with eleven magnified stars, each circled by dashes of silvery paint. A nebula sweeps in like a dragon, dodging the stars and curling around a second, smaller nebula. These two speeding spirals are separated from the mountaintops beneath them by a long stream of mysterious yellow light. The brightest member of the firmament is the sun, eclipsed by an orange moon. Van Gogh weds the moon and sun into one. The ribbon of mountains below this eerie heaven shelters fields and a town. Two cypress trees, painted with brown outlines, rise up on the left, their tendrils corkscrewing toward the highest star.

Reaching for the Heavens

As van Gogh painted the picture, the sky was the most important part in his mind. He might have been recalling the Old Testament story of Joseph, who saw eleven stars and the sun and moon bowing down to him, a tale the artist knew well. The village is typically Dutch, but the landscape is the familiar one around Saint-Rémy. Like the trees, the spire of the church reaches for the heavens.

Many consider this van Gogh's finest painting, even though its meaning is elusive. The subject is unique, but the reason for the painting's fame is its emotional intensity. Painted in a high pitch of religious fervor, it stands out as one of the great spiritual works of the nineteenth century.

OVERLEAF:
While spinning stars and swirling comets transfigure the sky, no one seems to be present to witness the strange occurrence. Lighted windows indicate that the villagers are indoors. Van Gogh painted their houses and the church with rigid, angular lines that contrast with the flowing curves above.

First Steps, after Millet

Van Gogh's Hero

While van Gogh was in the hospital, he decided to make painted copies of Jean-François Millet's prints. Millet was his idol. Born poor in rural France thirty-nine years before van Gogh, this famous artist painted peasants most of his life. When van Gogh first saw a large exhibition of drawings by Millet in Paris, he was deeply inspired. In a letter to Theo, he wrote that he should have said to himself, "Take off your shoes, for the place where you are standing is Holy Ground." His opinion of the man never changed; to him, Millet was "the greatest of the greats." Van Gogh always tried to emulate the "truth and simplicity" of this artist's work. He even called him "Father Millet."

Black-and-white prints of Millet's paintings were popular during van Gogh's lifetime. Van Gogh owned a few dozen of them, and had photographs of Millet's works as well. He valued these images greatly because he felt that the human soul—which he called "a precious pearl"—was visible in Millet's art. Van Gogh learned to draw people by copying figures from the prints, making them into large sketches.

Adding Color

Transferring the peasant subjects from prints to canvas was comforting, and van Gogh completed more than a dozen such paintings. He let each print "pose . . . as a subject," as if the printed piece of paper were a person or a vase of flowers. By making these paintings, van Gogh felt he was helping Millet, whose death almost five years earlier meant he had "had no time to paint [these] in oil." Using a traditional method called scoring to copy the prints onto canvas, van Gogh made fairly exacting versions of Millet's designs. First, he drew a grid, or checkerboard pattern, on a print and on a canvas. Each had the same number of squares. It was much easier and more accurate to copy the part of the

Jean-François Millet
FIRST STEPS

image that was in each small square one at a time onto the canvas than to copy the whole painting at once. This was done with pencil. Painting in the colors was the last task, and it gave van Gogh great joy. "My brush goes between my fingers as a bow would on the violin, and absolutely for my own pleasure," he wrote. The paintings were so different from the black-and-white prints that the artist concluded that his task was "much more translating them into another tongue than copying them."

First Steps
Van Gogh's brother Theo married "a good Dutch girl" who was called Jo. Soon she was expecting a child. As a gift to them, van Gogh decided to copy a charming scene of a young family by Millet called *First Steps*. "How beautiful that Millet is," he exclaimed upon seeing the photograph of it he had ordered. He scored it, copied it onto canvas with pencil, and then began enhancing it with colors that were new and unusual for him—soft, creamy greens, sun-washed yellows, whites, and blues.

What was not unusual for van Gogh was the way he put on the paint. For trees and bushes, he twisted his brush to make spirals. Small, wavy motions of his hand resulted in the earth of the vegetable garden and the thatched roofs of the farm buildings. Darker lines around the edges of the three figures made them stand out. The outlines of the wheelbarrow were filled in with

touches of tan and green paint. Van Gogh sent his painting to his brother and sister-in-law as soon as it was dry. A son was born on January 31, 1890, and they named him Vincent Willem. When van Gogh's stay in the Saint-Rémy asylum was over, he hurried to Paris to see his namesake.

Van Gogh selected pastel colors because he thought this painting might hang in the new baby's nursery. In his letters, van Gogh mentioned Millet more than any other artist, respecting his ability to picture peasants as noble human beings.

Crows over a Wheatfield

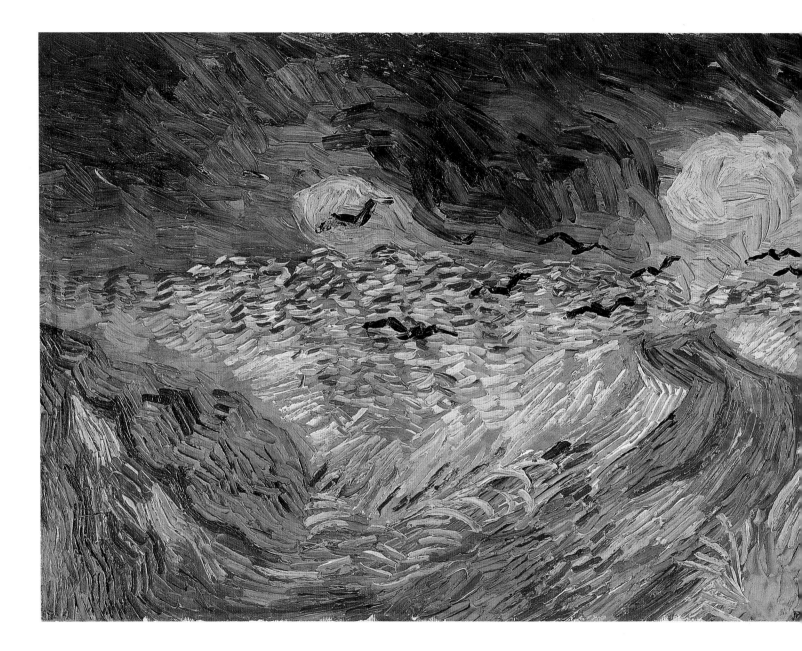

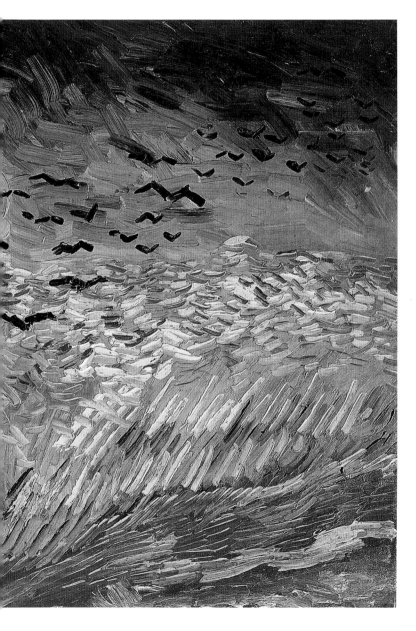

Van Gogh liked his sister-in-law and was happy to be in the midst of the new family. He also got to visit Père Tanguy and other old friends.

Just an hour's journey outside of Paris, on the river Oise, was the quiet town of Auvers, where he decided to live. Going to bed at nine most nights, and rising at five so he could catch a full day's light for painting, van Gogh led a disciplined life. He completed about one canvas a day. This speed, he explained, was "to express the desperately rapid passing of things in modern life." The thatched cottages of Auvers, falling into ruin, were one of those "things," so he painted them to record their appearance before they were gone forever. The modern villas, the church, the fields and farms were other subjects. He also found interesting people to paint.

Above Auvers was a seemingly endless plateau of wheatfields spreading to the horizon. Van Gogh wanted to capture the vastness of the scene, so he chose a canvas twice as wide as it was tall. When he got to the site, a storm was brewing and he saw a fast-changing scene in front of him. In his painting, black crows hurry to

Van Gogh's boldly painted expanses of blue and gold converge with stripes of red and green. The large marks of his brush bring these four regions of color together into a restless composition.

find shelter. The sun shines above the wheat, making it glow like gold as the wind bends it to the ground. Echoing the shapes of the crows, strokes of deep red make wavelike marks across the ocean of wheat to show how it ripples. To paint the scene, van Gogh stood just about at the intersection of three lanes cut into the field by farm carts to plant and harvest. He called attention to the red-clay color of the dirt lanes by painting margins of weeds on either side of them in bright green, their complementary color. The long, wavy lines he used to show the weeds and the lanes seem to flow like rivers toward the bottom of the canvas, where they join into one road.

Van Gogh painted a number of views of the wheatfields above Auvers and was eager to show them to Theo. He wrote his brother that he saw "health and restorative forces" in the countryside. While the storm in *Crows over a Wheatfield* appears to some viewers as an omen of van Gogh's death, he himself saw the golden wheat as an affirmation of life.

A Final Home

Two months after he moved to Auvers, van Gogh shot himself with a pistol. He died two days later, on July 29, 1890. Why Vincent van Gogh committed suicide will never be known, but the day before he died, his brother Theo, who had hurried from Paris to be at his side, said, "He feels so alone." It is not certain which of van Gogh's works was the last one he painted, but *Crows over a Wheatfield* was completed in the days just before his death.

Van Gogh was buried in a new cemetery on the edge of the wheatfields. Theo died six months later, and was buried next to his brother. His widow, Jo, took care of van Gogh's paintings and saved the hundreds of letters he had sent to Theo. She raised her son to honor his uncle as the greatest artist who ever lived. When Vincent Willem became an old man, he helped start the Vincent van Gogh Museum in Amsterdam. All of Vincent's paintings and drawings that Theo had accumulated during Vincent's brief life—and that Theo, Jo, and Vincent Willem had lovingly preserved—were passed on to the museum. It was van Gogh's gift to the people of the world.

IRISES

What Makes a van Gogh

Van Gogh's paintings are filled with bold color and vivid pattern.

1.

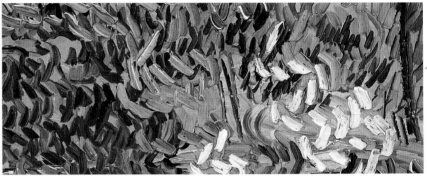

4.

2.

5.

3.

1. He placed complementary colors next to one another to increase their power.

2. He laid down thick layers of paint.

3. Van Gogh created shadows and reflections with a combination of colors, not just with black.

4. His brushstrokes are vigorous and form strong patterns.

5. Van Gogh outlined his figures to make them stand out against the background.

a van Gogh?